Division Street

DIVISION STREET

Arthur Bull

First Edition

Hidden Brook Press
www.HiddenBrookPress.com
writers@HiddenBrookPress.com

Copyright © 2019 Hidden Brook Press
Copyright © 2019 Arthur Bull

All rights for poems revert to the author. All rights for book, layout and design remain with Hidden Brook Press. No part of this book may be reproduced except by a reviewer who may quote brief passages in a review. The use of any part of this publication reproduced, transmitted in any form or by any means, electronic, mechanical, photocopied, recorded or otherwise stored in a retrieval system without prior written consent of the publisher is an infringement of the copyright law.

Division Street
by Arthur Bull

Cover Design – Richard M. Grove
Layout and Design – Richard M. Grove

Typeset in Cambria
Printed and bound in Canada
Distributed in USA by Ingram,
　　in Canada by Hidden Brook Distribution

Library and Archives Canada Cataloguing in Publication

Title: Division Street / Arthur Bull.
Names: Bull, Arthur, 1950- author.
Description: First edition. | Poems.
Identifiers: Canadiana (print) 20190153466 | Canadiana (ebook) 20190153474 |
ISBN 9781927725788 (softcover) | ISBN 9781927725795 (EPUB) |
ISBN 9781927725801 (Kindle)
Classification: LCC PS8553.U4675 D58 2019 | DDC C811/.54—dc23

For
Ruth Mary Bull

Contents

Wave Theory – *p. 7*
School – *p. 8*
Some Things We Didn't Know – *p. 12*
Softball – *p. 14*
The Park Theatre – *p. 15*
Spacemaster X-7 – *p. 16*
Terror – *p. 20*
Poe – *p. 22*
Ambrose – *p. 26*
Hideouts – *p. 27*
Lake Ontario – *p. 28*
Politics – *p. 33*
Port Hope Drive-In – *p. 34*
Division Street – *p. 36*
Jokeland – *p. 37*
The Cold War – *p. 38*
defense – *p. 42*
Lampreys – *p. 44*
Empire – *p. 45*
Past Wars – *p. 46*
Colonialism – *p. 49*
Rice Lake – *p. 50*
The Last Horse – *p. 51*
Safe Harbour – *p. 52*
Translating Aeschylus – *p. 53*
After School – *p. 54*
Valentine's Day – *p. 55*

Beatniks – *p. 56*
The Senators – *p. 57*
Talking Horses – *p. 58*
Cubs – *p. 60*
The Breakers – *p. 62*
The Duke of Earl – *p. 67*
Ranger 7 – *p. 68*
Bad Decisions – *p. 69*
Another Day – *p. 70*
Bad Songs – *p. 71*
The Shoop Shoop Song – *p. 72*

Acknowledgements – *p. 75*
A Short Author Bio – *p. 77*

*If a man could pass thro' Paradise in a Dream,
and have a flower presented to him
as a pledge that his Soul had really been there,
and found that flower in his hand when he awoke,
– Aye? What then?*

Samuel Taylor Coleridge

*The power of things inheres in the memories
they gather up inside them,
and also in the vicissitudes of our imagination,
and our memory—of this there is no doubt."*

Orhan Pamuk

*Fair seed-time had my soul, and I grew up
Foster'd alike by beauty and by fear*

William Wordsworth

Wave Theory

In the winter along the beach
waves would freeze
coat after coat of spray with each
layer layering
accumulation where shapes
rose, Baroque
monsters slippery and ornate
as memory itself.
We'd climb them to slide down,
no foot- or hand-
hold, helplessly drawn forward
into the breakers.

School

I

Everything we learned was contained in lists:
La Vérendrye, Champlain, Mackenzie, Thompson,
Fraser, Cabot, Frobisher, Cartier,
Northumberland, Dufferin, Lennox, Haldimand,
Brant, Middlesex, Simcoe, Frontenac,
stamen, pistil, petal, filament,
sepal, St. Lawrence, Mackenzie, Fraser,
Athabaska, head, thorax, abdomen.
Speed was more important than knowledge,
racing through timetables and spelling bees,
litanies rhymed off, carried with breathless
rapidity, as though there would come a time
in our lives when we'd find we had nothing
but names, and names alone could save us.

II

Our reader was called *High Flight,*
with all the usual anthology pieces
(poems by Maesfield, Frost, Houseman)
 as well as some Canadian pieces:

A poem by Wilfred Campbell
that stated 'the hour before the flush of dawn'
[laughing behind our hands]

And one by Duncan Campbell Scott
with the line 'The hawks fell twanging from the sky'
[like Duane Eddy's guitar?]

An essay by Vincent Massey
on being a Canadian:
'touch of breeziness and an alertness
that suggest the new world'
[really???]

It had colour plates of paintings
by the Group of Seven:

The Red Maple by AY Jackson
*[daydreaming: looking through black tree
  branches into a world of red leaves fluttering
  over churning rapids]*

Northern River by Tom Thompson
[daydreaming: mesh of branches,: distant touch of colour reflected on river, bending far away]

One section called 'Growing Up In Canada '
began with a drawing of a young man
attempting to scale a sheer vertical rock face
in the middle of a barren treeless wilderness
[yes, that sounded about right]

III

Where you sit in class is important,
amidst all the flying projectiles,
undercurrents of whispers,
and passing of notes, the mayhem
Rocks in the very back, who hung out
at Cortese's Pool Hall after school,
who could open up pop bottles
with her teeth. In the front, girls
from rich families: doctors'
and lawyers' daughters, nicely
dressed, full of gossip, stuck up,
desirable. In the middle, the rest
of us: kids from up north
(Bewdley, Gore's Landing, Roseneath,
Warkworth) and kids from the Rez,
at Rice Lake, my walking-to-school
friend from the Hoo-Lee Gardens.
And girls with names like Stinkweed
(my crush) and Mudcat, who flirted
with the Rocks. And right in front of me,
every morning the girl from the only
Jewish family in town who stood silently
during the Lord's Prayer, in what
seemed to me to be a silent halo.

Some Things We Didn't Know

That smoking is bad for you. In fact we went from stronger to stronger brands: Black Cat, Sweet Caporal, Export A and finally Old Port Cigarillos, even though they made us sick. Once we even smoked punk wood that we found growing near the lake.

That X-rays are dangerous. We used to stop at the shoe store on the way home at lunchtime to put our feet in the x-ray machine and look at our feet bones, and once I had a Plantar's Wart that was removed by a huge x-ray gun operated by a man in a lead suit. The wart fell off within a day.

That the CIA had murdered Patrice Lumumba, President of the Democratic Republic of Congo.

That some children in our classrooms were often seriously harmed by their own parents

That the last Lake Ontario salmon was caught in 1898, after which they became extinct.

That the RCAF firebombed Hamburg and Dresden.

That Duncan Campbell Scott, whose poem beginning with the line 'Last night a storm fell on the world' was in our reader, was also the Deputy Minister of the Department of Indian Affairs, and the main architect of the residential schools policy.

That some kids in our class were being taken away from their families by the government, and sent to residential schools.

That we were in someone else's place, and that their descendants were among our classmates.

Softball

Saturday summer evenings,
we'd go down to the lake
to watch the girls' softball.
The games were long and relaxed,
slow-paced, almost languorous.
We went to watch the pitchers,
each one with her own unique style:
the baroque wind-up, the eccentric
underhand turn and release
with a curlicue twist, the knee dip
then slightest shake of the head.
Through the heat and murmur
of conversation the occasional
cheer or jeer from the stands.
From the Pav, music on the PA
warming up for the dance later
drifted across the vague wash
of surf through the summer night:
the sound of the Shirelles singing
I've been told when a boy kiss a girl,
take a trip around the world.

The Park Theatre

Saturday matinee at the Park Theatre,
soon to become a thing of the past,
showing whatever reels were still making
the small town Ontario movie circuit.

Old dusters, Warner Bros cartoons,
sometimes even real oldies
from '40s like *My Friend Flicka*
The movies didn't really matter.

They were only the backdrop
for the pandemonium in the seats:
popcorn boxes flying through the air,
everyone yelling at top of their lungs,

Sometimes the din got so bad
the manager would turn off the projector
and threaten to stop the movie altogether
"If yous kids don't behave..."

And the crabby usher with her flashlight.
And somewhere in the middle, oblivious,
a boy and girl could feel the once and only
sweetness of just holding hands.

Spacemaster X-7

I

A space probe returns to earth covered
with a mysterious fungus that transforms
into an ever-growing pile of space rust
that, when accidentally tinged with human blood,
became Bloodrust, threatening to cover the earth.

II

The idea of uncontrollably toxic
substances was quite familiar to us.
How Factory Creek flowed bright orange
from the General Wire and Cable Company,
and the mountains of emerald green
algae blooms, larded with dead smelts,
so thick they slowed the waves.

III

In front of the General Foods plant (Cobourg's biggest
a thriving product of Ontario's branchplant economy)
they had a huge sign that said GENERAL FOODS
HOME OF JELL-O, hence known as *The Jell-O Factory*.
For us, it was important for another reason altogether:
in each box of *Jell-O* they put a free hockey coin,
a little plastic disc holding a photo of an NHL player
like a Russian icon, they were all there: Sawchuk,
Mahovolich, Howe, Keon, Baun, Shack, Bower, Hull
Geoffrion, Belliveau, Lafleur and the Rocket.
For a time, they were the main schoolyard currency.
So it was a huge discovery to learn that General Foods
was dumping massive amounts of unsold *Jell-O*
in the woods behind the plant, including hockey coins.
When we got there, we found that the boxes had mostly
been dissolved by rain leaving a huge mountain
of pastel coloured sludge that we waded through
in rubber boots, picking out the coins by the hundreds.

IV

When we hiked to Port Hope we'd pass
Eldorado Mining and Refining,
where they refined the uranium
for the Manhattan Project, and all
the early atomic bombs, and buried,
some say, half a million cubic metres
of radioactive waste around the town
in parks, fields, ravines, the harbour
and even in the material that people
used to build their houses with.
We had no idea how close we were
to history which, like radiation,
is everywhere, and always invisible.

Terror

Most people flee in terror before the part of themselves that is impersonal.
                Giorgio Agaben

The point about fear was to be fearless.
We sought out the most dangerous places
we could find. Hearing rumours about a kid
getting drowned in Factory Creek,
swept away in the spring flood, we went
right away with ropes to cross hand-over-hand
above the rushing water. Or walked across
the railway bridge high above Port Hope
never pausing, deliberately not knowing
the train schedule, walking very slowly,
glancing sideways at each other, knowing
you could never ever lose your nerve.
Or climbing up the pigeon-shit-covered
warped ladder in the St Peter's church tower
past the huge bronze bells (hoping
no one would come and start playing them)
get out at the top and dance on the parapets
high above King Street (I could not watch).
Or swim in Pratt's pond with the double fear
of lamprey eels fastening their round sharp
teeth-filled mouths onto our bodies
or being sucked down over the dam
beside the motionless mill wheel,
water smacking down on the concrete
twenty feet below. We sought it out.

Or someone bringing his dad's .22
and a box of bullets and shooting up things
out in the middle of nowhere somewhere.
We were lucky there was no war on,
When they need large numbers of boys like us,
as yet unacquainted with fear of death.

Poe

There is no exquisite beauty... without some strangeness in the proportion.
        Edgar Allen Poe

I

Of course the patron saint of all this fear
was Poe. Not the Poe of Baudelaire's
bad dreams or Mallarme's hydras and angels
but Corman's Poe, from Universal Studios,
a combination of high artifice, creepy
slapstick and menace, with a cast of ageing stars
from the heyday of horror, whose careers
were now in full decline, enjoying themselves:
Vincent Price, overripe and unctuous,
Peter Lorre, who could make any sentence
an insinuation, and the grim formalities
of Karloff and Rathbone, their huge
personalities easily overpowering
poor Corman and even Poe. Like when
Vincent Price asks *Shall I ever see the rare
and radiant Lenore again?* The Raven
(Lorre) answers How the hell should I know?

II

Between St. Peter's and the rectory there was a crypt
the size of a small garage, dark, discoloured cement,
moss-covered, cracked all over, with no visible entry.
The old caretaker of the church, a Barnardo Boy, told us
that in fact we were right: there was a tunnel
from somewhere in the church basement, but nobody
remembered where. So we spent hours with flashlights
crawling through passageways so narrow
you had to turn sideways, always bricked up,
always with the theremin soundtrack in our ears
from Premature Burial and Ray Milland's
overwrought voice, the memory of painted scenery,
and the opening graveyard scene, so fake and yet so real.

III

Some Words
from *Tales of Terror*
I didn't know
when I was 12,
and that I still
do not know today:
Curricle
Copper-stick
Distrain
Fantod
Dolorfuge
Finger-post
Galluses
Ignis-Fatuus
Thirtover
Wherry

IV

The Rochester Ferry Dock, now
a memory in the mind of the harbour,
pilings reduced to broken stumps
slimed with bright green seaweed.

Once it brought visitors from the USA
every single day. I tried to picture it:
ladies with parasols, helped down
the gangplank by gentlemen friends,

Travelling, tradesmen with satchels
full of samples to sell in Ontario,
tourist groups organized by Kiwanis
and perhaps among them, a man,

Short, dark complexion, fine featured
humming with a distracted air, holding
a black briefcase monographed in gold
with his initials : Mr. E.A. Poe.

Ambrose

As a little kid I had an extreme fear of dogs
and, for some reason (this was probably why),
I was given the job of looking after the new dog,
a bulldog named Ambrose, (after the saint).
To say Ambrose was flawed would be serious
understatement. He was a dog afflicted
with multiple diseases and bad habits
all of which he carried like a badge of honour.
Infected ears, running fluids, a 'double eyelid'
that made a white bubble under one eye,
farting and drooling without pause,
able to leg-fuck at a moment's notice,
so ugly that once some American tourists
stopped their car to tell me that I should
put such an dangerous animal on a leash.
He was the perfect expression of the shock
 and wonderment of embodiment itself,
and was everything I could want in a dog.
Once, when we were painting the garage
green, one of my friends dabbed the paintbrush
on his balls creating a spectacle both indelible
and unmentionable that he happily
presented to the Ladies Auxiliary tea
and other church-related gatherings.

Hideouts

Children take a particular pleasure in hiding,
not because they will be found in the end,
but by the very act of hiding
Giorgio Agaben

We had little hideouts tucked away
　everywhere around town.

Climbing up the highest pine tree
to boards nailed to swaying boughs
holding tight, hands sticky with sap.

Inside a collapsed cement foundation
squeezing through a narrow crack
not knowing if we could come back out.

Walking the diving board above
an old empty swimming pool
behind an abandoned mansion.

Secret passageways inside the walls
of St.Peter's, the organ pipe room,
peepholes to the sanctuary.

Crawling into hollows inside thickets
　where you could smoke, and maybe,
just maybe, sometime meet...girls!

Lake Ontario

I

Other Possible Names for the Lake

As well as the many
reliable names
given to the lake:

Lake Ontario,
Lac Frontenac,
Niigaani-gichigami
(Leading Sea)
Gichi-zaaga'igan,
(Big Lake]
(Lake of Shining Waters)
Oniatarío:io
(Beautiful Lake)
or Skaniatarí:io,
or Oniarà:ke

Various other names
have been proposed
but rejected over
the years, including:
Tired Duck Lake

Liver Lake
(because of the shape)
Le lac du lac
Junior Lake
Lake Aubergine
Lake-Forget-Your-Own-Name
Lake Boredom

II

Lake Sturgeon are huge fish,
10 to 15 feet long, twice
 as long as full grown man,
weighing almost half a ton.
Once so abundant and abundantly
caught in incidental fisheries
they piled up on shore to dry
and burned, fed to pigs, spread
as fertilizer, stacked like cordwood
or used to fuel for steamboats.
Over 5 million pounds taken
in one year. The stocks collapsed
by 1900, and never recovered.

III

In the summer
you could spend
all day at the beach
alternating between
baking on the sand,
run-diving into
huge breakers
and occasionally
going for fries
at the Pav. Once
I burned so bad
I could hardly bend
my knees. That night
we went to see
Lawrence of Arabia
at the Park Theatre:
a kind of perfect
alignment of art
and suffering.
The scene where
Omar Sharif
rode his camel
towards the oasis
starting as a speck
on the horizon
(one of the most
famous long-

shots of all time)
and took forever
to cross the burning
sand, so hot and slow.
I had not yet read
Lawrence's essay
on guerilla warfare
(*Encyclopedia Britannica*
1905 edition,
still definitive.)

That same summer
we were learning
the meaning of new
words : 'insurgents'
'communist rebels'
'military observers'
and a new place
called Vietnam.

Politics

Politics, another bizarre preoccupation
of adults, would make its appearance
from time to time in the life of the town.
Dief came during an election campaign
to made a speech at the Pav. As he left,
I shook his hand, and remember wondering
how someone that profoundly unattractive
could be the Prime Minister of Canada.
Sometimes there were election rallies
that they would pack with school kids.
Once we were sent by bus to Kingston
to hear Pearson speak in the hockey arena.
Suddenly, right in middle of his speech,
a crowd of Tories, who'd been strategically
positioned around the stage, pulled out
their signs, started waving them and yelling
slogans, until they were strong-armed outside.
Politics was very similar to the carnie
that came about once a year every summer:
the freak show, the girlie show, dodgy rides,
cotton candy and many kinds of toss games
with prizes of giant pink stuffed animals.

Port Hope Drive-In

I

If you go straight north of the Drive-In
first you cross fields of reddish dirt
ploughed by tiny tractors trailing plumes
of dust-drawn parallels in the distance,
then over eskers and drumlins shaped
by a recent glacier's slow hand turning
like a potter's, rolling side to side,
dragging its body's leisurely retreat,
then over Rice Lake named for wild rice
sustainer of life, called *manoomin* (not
rice at all) then to the Serpent Mounds,
the winding hills that hold of the bones
who sing this place's future and its past.

II

At the Drive-In, what's showing is *The Siege of Syracuse*
Italian sword-and-sandals about the Roman invasion
of Sicily in 214 BC. It includes the story of Archimedes
who was working for the King of Sicily at the time
of the Roman conquest, that very same Archimedes
inventor of the heat ray, the screw pump, the giant claw,
who discovered many geometrical theorems including
how to find the surface area and volume of a sphere,
the volume of an irregular shaped object and, most beautifully,
how you get the area of a circle (multiplying
π times the square of its radius.) That same Archimedes
  was inscribing diagrams in the dust in his courtyard
when Roman soldiers entered and ordered him to come
and report to the victorious Roman general Marcellus,
to which he replied, it is said: "Do not disturb my circles",
for which he was murdered, right then and there.

Division Street

Is always one of those places
where my dreams happen,
no matter what else the dream
is about I end up here
walking down Division Street
toward Victoria Park,
past the white bandshell
where the Kiltie Band plays,
past the slow motion ballet
of the Lawn Bowling Club
and down to the harbour,
the coal heaps, the pier,
right down to the lake
always awaiting my arrival
waiting there, so flat and grey.
But it never occurs to me,
even once, to ask where
the division lay, and what
it was that was being divided.

Jokeland

Our trips to Toronto invariably
took us to our favourite store,
Jokeland on Yonge Street,
where we would pick up supplies
of joke material: rubber vomit,
plastic dog turd, fake melted ice-cream
whatever we needed for our projects.
In the back it had an ADULT area
with a large array of dildos,
plastic buttocks and hats with tits.
We treated these items with caution
understanding them as another
inexplicable adult preoccupation.

The Cold War

I

During the Cuban Missile Crisis
a girl ran home at recess in tears.
Adults were talking to children
about the very real possibility
of *everyone* being burned alive.
We took this all in our stride,
since we'd seen the great Kaiju
monster movies at the Park.
We knew what would happen,
the way crowds would flee
looking over their shoulders,
as they ran toward the camera,
the wind from Mothra's wings
collapsing bridges and buildings,
Godzilla advancing, unstoppable,
through smoke of burning cities
(himself the result of nuclear war)
and how the world was fragile,
crafted, meticulous and delicate,
of rice paper, string and cardboard.

II

They put a map in the front entrance called Danger Zones.
Every week a teacher would update it in bright red,

Naming places in the world where there was trouble:
Cuba, Berlin, Algeria, Kenya, The Belgian Congo.

Places to worry about– as if worrying were something
important– hotspots of anxiety, but far enough away

To be ignored, since none were in North America, where
there were no burning cities or assassinations yet.

III

New names and new characters moved
through our daily lives, half-heard,
not yet passed down into history
as shadowy characters waiting in the wings.
each name a knot in a terrible plot line:
Patrice Lumumba, Adolf Eichmann,
Fidel Castro, Nikita , Khruschev, Gary Power,
We added them to our mythologies
where they took their places among
the other characters in Harryhausens's
stop-action in *7th Voyage of Sinbad*,
alongside Snake Woman and Skeleton Warrior.

IV

Dew Line Duty was the first novel
I can remember reading right through
(I was a slow reader and rarely finished
one, even stopping the *Jungle Book*.)

The hero, Dale of the Mounted,
was sent to investigate Russian spies
who were infiltrating the DEW Line
the Distant Early Warning defense,

A system of radar stations Up North
to detect incoming Soviet bombers.
The spies were hiding amongst
a boatload of refugees from Hungary

Which even then seemed a little unlikely.
Dale was no mastermind, not someone
you were supposed to be afraid of,
just a guy doing the job of saving Canada.

defense

I

No one explained why was there was nothing orange
in the Orange Parade. Only later information
would fill it in: King Billy on this white horse,
Papist plots, the Battle of the Boyne, the hanging
of Riel. Still it was puzzling, and also: how
could those musicians in the marching band play
clarinets and trumpets wearing woolen gloves.

II

Lodge
peel
County
Crush
juice
Blossom (Special)
jump suit
Revolution
Parade

Lampreys

The lamprey is a monster
with a round mouth
lined with razor-sharp
teeth, slithering
through the darkness,
an undulating muscle
capable of attachment
to the human body
capable of sucking
blood from your body
deep down there below
where we went swimming
near the old mill wheel
out at Pratt's Pond.

Empire

You were caught between two empires—
one fading and one coming on strong.
Our spellers said *aeroplane* and *programme*,
we pledged allegiance to the British Empire
every morning and pink areas on the roll-up
map of the world that told us how once
we had belonged to some exotic empire
an imperial dream, now dusty and tattered.
When the Queen came we sat on the curb
In flannel shorts with little union Jacks
knowing something had already gone past.
At the same time we sensed the Americans
were closing in on us from every direction.
We weren't sure about them, like monsters,
dangerous and likable at the same time.
(But we knew that they were not infallible–
we'd heard about Sputnik and Bay of Pigs).
Our main weapon against them was derision:
Sea Hunt (Lloyd Bridges parting seaweed)
Highway Patrol (Broderick Crawford
climbing painfiully out of his patrol car),
Jet Jackson, Davy Crockett. Sky King,
sent us into fits of laughter and parody.
But derision did not always work: westerns
were harder because the heroes were guys
like Steve McQueen in *Wanted Dead or Alive*
Chuck Connor (the razor jaw) *The Rifleman*,
Clint Eastwood in *Rawhide*, Richard Boone
as smooth Paladin in *Have Gun Will Travel*.
Against men as cool and merciless as these
we knew we probably didn't stand a chance.

Past Wars

I

For a peaceful small town there was a lot of war,
mostly under the long shadow of WWII
that hung over us the way Waterloo
must have hung over the Victorians.

'Bombs on Tokyo!' we'd yell, jumping down
like the bombardiers over Tokyo yelling
"Geronimo!" as they let go their payloads,
(100,000 civilians in a single night).

They were calling the name of the great
Chiricahua general who led his people
in resistance to the United States of America
in the Apache Wars only 60 years before.

II

An elderly bachelor who lived on Division Street
had been a sergeant in the British army,
Like a minor character out of Kipling,
and fought in many of the empire's wars:
Boer War, Boxer Rebellion, Northwest Rebellion,
Gallipoli, Iraq, the Irish Uprising, Sudan.
When he died they had a lawn sale, a dream-like
collection of objects from distant worlds
spread out on the grass: sabres, flags,
lances, pith helmets, rugs, cushions, samovars
I managed to get a shillelagh with a lead core
and I never once stopped to consider
how many skulls it had actually cracked.

III

What did those words mean? *Ortona
Dieppe, the Scheldt Estuary,
Caen, Falaise Gap?* What
secrets did these foreign places hold?
The ribbons and scars of our fathers
and uncles meant little to us, seldom
spoken of except in the distance,
their long shadows hanging over:
the drone of an air raid siren,
buried far away, yet always present.
The absent-minded fingers
tapping out of morse code
messages at the dinner table.

Colonialism

Every show was brought to you
by a sponsor. *Death Valley Days*,
brought to you by 20 Mule Team Borax,
Bonanza, brought to you by Chevrolet
Perry Como brought to you by Kraft
(recipes with mini-marshmallows)
Sky King brought to you by Peter Pan
Peanut Butter, *Superman* by Kelloggs.
Apparently nothing could happen
without first being brought to you
by some greater distant power.

Rice Lake

One weekend we discovered the rail bed
of the Cobourg and Peterborough Railway
that was built to go up north to Rice Lake,
connecting Cobourg with Peterborough.
It was barely there– no rails, no ties,
a raised scar running through the woods
over eskers and drumlins like a welt
along the forest floor, with nothing to say
it held up train tracks except for
its straightness. How strange, we thought,
having only just arrived here,
that we already had our own ruins.

The Last Horse

It should have been forty years earlier
that horse-drawn milk wagons
were on their way out but there it was,
as though transported from another age
onto our street for one last run.
We were sent out with sugar cubes
to feed the horse, the last horse,
somehow sensing the sense of occasion,
like Elvis coming to the Gardens
in Toronto, or a visit by the Queen.

As a child you are not small
to yourself, and your world is larger
than it ever will be again, but I felt small
beside that horse as it stood in our street
unblinking eyes behind leather blinders,
huge neck, curled back
lips, so soft on my little palm.
So long ago and yet so clear
in the late light of that afternoon
standing together, horse and boy,
in the heavy shadow of things gone by.

Safe Harbour

Safe Harbour we called it
because of the condoms
floating there Sunday
morning after Saturday
night's backseat love.
We climbed the coal heaps,
high-wired the booms,
shinnied down pilings
slick with green seaweed.
I heard, many years later,
long after we'd moved,
one of our gang got drowned
in there. I couldn't recall
his face as hard as I tried,
but I did recall the two
long arms of the piers
stretching out and bending
inwards as if closing
in a cold embrace.

Translating Aeschylus

When you are twelve and find a rabbit dead
the prize is the skin, you cut and I,
as younger brother, stood and watched
the spread of yellow green and red
like a map of countries. We didn't mind.
We acted in the cause of wildness.
And now into this stubborn Greek
that picture rises and the words
rise again in their roughness
from the page– the thousand ships,
storm clouds, the two-fold power
put forth from the shore,
the sign of the hare, torn by the eagle
the sign of the unborn devoured by dogs–
all mixed up in my bad translation.
Now you are a country away
and dreaming back through ancient Greece
I worry about you for the first time.

After School

Walking home from school
was all about performance:
buying cream puffs
at Andrews Bakery
(ammo for food fights),
teaching mynah bird
 in Stedmans 5 and 10
how to say 'fuck off',
walking like Egyptians
past the barbershop
window. But sometimes
I'd walk by myself
along the street behind
King Street, by the back
entrances of the stores
and restaurants, somehow
a secret, quiet way home,
along a different street,
where new and secret things
were folded into shadows.

Valentine's Day

The teachers put a little mailbox
beside each classroom door
like a ballot box only with cupids
and hearts. On the given signal
(the bell) we streamed out
into the halls to deliver our cards
to our secret loves, mostly
anonymously, but with broad clues,
(strictly in keeping with the tradition).
Suddenly on that day Central School
became a festival of love, electrified
by the thrill of someone asking you,
someone you might not even know
asking you, secretly, *Will you be mine?*

Beatniks

We knew about beatniks,
in fact we thought we *were*
beatniks, wandering around
Victoria Park, reciting dreamy
beatnik poems we'd made up.
One began with the sea
is a cow. Another went:
Mingus, Mingus, Mingus,
wearing berets and fake
Goatees, We were children.
How could we know that we
were in fact getting ready
for the rest of our lives?

The Senators

The old men on the bench
outside Victoria Hall
were called the Senators,
out of an uncertain mix
of respect and mockery.
One of them always wore
a three-piece suit, and never
seemed to say very much.
From time to time he wrote
in a small ringed notebook.
Maybe this was Kipling,
I wondered, misplaced now
in the wrong age and country,
on the edge of the wrong empire.
Occasionally he would take out
a gold watch from his waistcoat
fob pocket, checking the time.

Talking Horses

*A horse is a horse
of course, of course*
that tautology, followed
by the hoofbeat
repetition, that sets
us up for the contra-
distinctive *but*...
as if to say: *this*,
this is no ordinary
horse, but rather
this is *Mr Ed*, talking
horse, who could
not only speak but
also got all the jokes
at the expense of
his hapless owner.
He recalled the great
talking horses
of the past, starting
with Achilles' Xanthus
in the Iliad , and right
down to Dorn's
Talking Horse
in *Gunslinger*, laid-
back, laconic,
laced with LSD.
Kipling had one
in a short story,

but hardly worth noting
since he also had talking
steam engine and boats,
and every animal
he found In the jungle.
And all of them follow
one of the great unspoken
Rules of Literature:
If you do introduce
a talking horse,
you pretty well
have to give him
the last word.

Cubs

The meaning of 'woggle',
now lost to all but a few:
(a leather ring with a snap
on one side and wolf-
head on the other)
the only official way
of holding together
a scarf. Once a week
we would become wolf
cubs and dance
ritual wolf dances
following men
who'd become Balloo
the Bear and Akela
the Wolf (the postman
and the Churchwarden,
all World War II
veterans no doubt)
The Jungle Book
supplied us with totems
or the closest thing,
I pledge to do
my duty to God
and the Queen
and keep the law
of the wolf cub pack
and do a turn

to someone every day
[only one? I thought)
and once a week
there was a frantic search
for the woggle without
which nothing ever
would ever be held
together again.

The Breakers

I

Letters fading into stucco,
rundown villa-style apartments
once inviting genteel holidays,
now, a place to end up in,
with too many long hours,
filled with the drumming of the surf.

II

Once a door opened in it
that never opened before,
a lady beckoned, like a fairytale
witch, to me, out of all of us
shinny players. Whispered
in my ear, pressed some soft
folded bills into my palm,
something about rubbing alcohol
and the drugstore and be a good boy.
Her hand, holding mine,
was shaking. Later, lost
in a quandary, then in tears,
a simple transaction became
a moral crisis too much
for me to handle.

III

Waves are in fact circular
until they break against some shore
where each collapses on the next
dragging back its spent force to the lake,
pounding heart and gasping breath
In the winter the waves would freeze
one by one and pile up like mountains.
We'd slip and slide out to the edge
drawn by the romance of an icy turn

IV

I can still feel Lake Ontario's pull
and how the bills felt in my hand
and the force of the knowledge that,
that adults are not in control
of themselves or of the world

V

For such power to break itself and then re-form
all these waves of particles or selves
must serve up their brokenness to this world,
then freeze again as memory:
alone in the night with no comfort
except a drink and the memories
to go over again and again
until they feel the way ripples in the sand
feel to little bare feet, running.

The Duke of Earl

The year is 1962.
The place is Lake Baptiste
up in the Kawarthas.
Four twelve-year old
boys are paddling and singing
Duke of Earl to the rhythm
of their strokes, exhausted
tiny voices on the lake.
They have been told
they are going to David Milne's
cabin, the famous painter.
When they get there it's a ruin,
half-filled with porcupine shit.
Years later, at a show
of Milne's prints, I am drawn
not to the prints but to the plates
gouged and scored across
So they can't be repeated,
and every time I see one
of those finely etched landscapes
I remember, not the waves,
or the sunlight or the voices,
or all the lost memories,
but Gene Chandler's voice,
the way it soars above.

Ranger 7

The moon has to absorb so much
disappointment. In 1964
I remember the letdown at fourteen
when they came back with the photographs
of the far side (black and white,
grainy, same as this side).
It was not what I'd been counting on:
that everything would be different,
that everything would be unrecognizable
that they would all be at a loss
because even the dimensions
in which we are extended, that
make normal normal and real real,
would not be there and that
all our experiences would
have to be looked at new
we would have to start again
to make sense of this information.
Instead what we got was
the knowing reassurance
that it's the same as anywhere else,
as here. What we got was
this world and ourselves again
unchangeable, only further away.

Bad Decisions

The policy problems started early, in fact right at the beginning
with the misspelling of the name (one 'o' in Coburg)

And then the pointless rivalry with Port Hope that in turn led
to the building of a bridge over Rice Lake to ensure

that the railway to Peterborough didn't go from Port Hope,
built so poorly that it collapsed in a storm one night.

And right up to our time when the town fathers decided
to get rid of the rampant starling overpopulation

By making a recording of a starling having it leg twisted,
then having it played through loudspeakers

on a truck that drove slowly around the streets, blaring,
(the kind politicians used to use)

The starlings, although probably confused and angry,
apparently never did leave town.

Another Day

An ordinary day:
as usual we filed back
into school after recess,
boys through the boys door,
girls through the girls door,
jostling and fooling around,
but not so much as to attract
the attention of the duty teacher
who might send you to the Office,
where you could get the strap.
But there were no duty teachers-
they were all standing together
huddled at the top of the stairs,
and some of them were crying.
I remember thinking: what
thing could have happened
that would make the teachers cry.

Bad Songs

It was the Year of the Terrible Songs.
Chuck Berry was in jail, Elvis in the army,
Little Richard had joined the church.
What we got was the worst of the worst.

*Itsy bitsy teeny weeny yellow polkadot bikini
One-Eyed three-horned flying purple people eater,
Oo-ee-oo-ah-ah I asked the witch doctor
Oo ee oo ah ah ting tang walla walla bing bang
Who put the bomp in the bompshu omp shu omp*

Everyone knew how terrible it all was,
so terrible that it even made
Chubby Checker sound good.

But in amongst them there were some gems:
The Shirelles, early Miracles, the Marvelettes

And what we didn't know was
what they were getting us ready for:

The opening chords and then the words
that would change everything forever:

*Oh yeah,
I'll
tell you something
I hope you'll understand.*

The Shoop Shoop Song

A car backfires in the parking lot
faking a gunshot, and a flicker

Crosses the Tim Horton's, riding radio
waves that hold some simulacra

Of Betty Everett's voice, at once both
perfect and temporary, maintaining

It's in his kiss with some authority,
in fact insisting on it. I*s it in his eyes?*

Oh no, you'll be deceived. Is it in his sighs?
He'll make believe. (The instrumental

Break, a weirdly detached marimba solo)
Is it in his face? No, no that's just his charm

In his warm embrace? No, that's just his arm.
Meanwhile, at my table I'm trying to make

A little sanctuary inside it all,
made out of a coffee, a newspaper

And someone's collected poems. The world
presses in and I can't press back.

She's singing about what's real, what's
in his kiss and everything I need

to know about being in love suddenly
is there – *bang*! – it becomes clear

That the kiss Betty Everett's singing about
is *my* kiss: it was *my* kiss that it was in.

Acknowledgements

Some of these poems have been previously published in the journals *The Alchemist, Descant and Memoir (and)*.

The author would like to thank, David Neil Lee, George Elliott Clarke, Richard Grove (Tai) for their encouragement and editorial support.

A Short Author Bio:

Arthur Bull lives on Digby Neck in the Bay of Fundy area of Nova Scotia. He has previously published four book-length collections of poetry, and four chapbooks, and his work has appeared in numerous Canadian and international journals.

His poems and translations from classical Chinese have appeared in numerous Canadian and US journals.

Arthur Bull is also a musician, and has been involved in the improvised music scene, touring and recording since the mid-1970's. His primary employment has been with small-scale fishermen's organizations at the local, national and international level.

www.ingramcontent.com/pod-product-compliance
Lightning Source LLC
Chambersburg PA
CBHW020145130526
44591CB00030B/228